C000085440

The Langu

The Language of Coats

Deirdre Hines

Deirdre Hines

Hi Shanta,
    Here is a copy of my book. I
hope you enjoy it. I am
resident in Donegal, N.W of Ireland,
but visit London regularly.
       Kind Regards,
            Deirdre

NEW ISLAND

THE LANGUAGE OF COATS
First published 2012
by New Island
2 Brookside, Dundrum Road, Dublin 14
www.newisland.ie

Copyright © Deirdre Hines, 2012
The author has asserted her moral rights.

PRINT ISBN: 978-1- 84840-165-5
EPUB ISBN: 978-1- 84840-166-2
MOBI ISBN: 978-1- 84840-167-9

All rights reserved. The material in this publication is protected by copyright law. Except as may be permitted by law, no part of the material may be reproduced (including by storage in a retrieval system) or transmitted in any form or by any means; adapted; rented or lent without the written permission of the copyright owner.

Typeset by New Island Books
Cover design by New Island Books
Cover Image © Oleg Oprisco/Trevillion Images
Printed in the EU by Bell & Bain Ltd., Glasgow

New Island received financial assistance from The Arts Council
(An Comhairle Ealaíon), Dublin, Ireland.

Deirdre Hines & New Island acknowledge the help and support of 'Writers' Week' and the Listowel Poetry Collection Competition, and its sponsor, Tim Costelloe of Profile Developments.

10 9 8 7 6 5 4 3 2 1

For the eternal muses that are James Alexander Connors,
tiger and les chevaliers

Contents

About the author

Deirdre Hines was born in Liverpool. She moved to Belfast shortly thereafter and from there to Letterkenny in County Donegal, where she now lives.

She graduated from Trinity College Dublin in 1989, with a double-honours degree in English and Theatre Studies. She was awarded a T.E.F.L certificate from Sheffield Polytechnic, and a Certificate in Equality Studies from UCD.

She has written several plays, of which Howling Moons, Silent Sons won the Stewart Parker Award for Best New Play in 1992. Pigsback Theatre Company produced it. She went on to write Ghost Acreage at Vixen Time for Passion Machine's 'Songs of the Reaper' Festival in 1994. Other plays include A Moving Destiny (1996) produced by Yew Theatre Company, and Dreamframe, produced for Fishamble's 'Y2K' Festival.

Plays for children include Golden Moon (1997) and Borrowed Days (1999), produced and performed by the children of Kilmacrennan National School, County Donegal. She received two Arts Council grants, in 1994 and 1998 respectively.

Deirdre was short-listed for the Patrick Kavanagh Poetry Award in 2010. She bettered that, winning the Listowel Poetry Collection competition in 2011 with the first six poems in this collection. She has had articles published in several magazines, including The Countryman, Ireland's Own and Escape.

She has held various posts, which have included being Playwright in Residence with the Verbal Arts Centre, Community Development Worker for Travellers, assistant Manager of the George and Pilgrim Hotel in Glastonbury, Sub Primary School Teacher in Scoil Colmcille, Letterkenny and freelance writer. This is her first published collection of poems.

Introduction

W hen I was asked to write a short introduction to this collection of poetry by the editor of New Island Books, I was taken somewhat aback. It is one thing to write Poetry, and quite another to outline in prose the reasons for so doing. Whether it is questions of subject matter, theme or prosody there are many and multifaceted answers to those very questions. However, if I were to pluck a single flower from that protean mass of inspirations and influences, I would have to travel back in time to a small prefab in Primary School.

A curious custom occurred at each and every break time. Those children who hadn't completed their homework would be made to kneel in front of the blackboard and stare at the numbers chalked on it, while the rest went out to play. Maths was invariably the subject that preceded the longed-for scramble on the concrete yard. The freedom of those kneeling on the cold linoleum floor was guaranteed if I recited Padraic Colum's 'An Old Woman of the Roads' without making any mistakes. As the habitual homework offenders were two sisters who lived in a caravan outside the school gates, I thought the teacher chose the poem to make them feel better. It took maturity to realise the meaning of dramatic irony. The woman in the poem longed for a little house. The casual cruelty of such emphasis on their difference bothered me for many years. Still, I received many sweets and much friendship for my early role of poet-solicitor.

If it was in that classroom that I learned of the power of the poet, it was also in primary school that I learned of the importance of the performance. And, perhaps even more importantly, of the languages that exist outside of the small, printed shape of the poem; how the most nuanced, crafted pieces can be read and used in many different ways.

Inveigling my father to be what would now be called the designated driver, I became a Feis junkie, hopping from Derry Feis to Londonderry Feis in pursuit of the shining medals that were hung around my neck, like a gladiator returning triumphant from the ring. And what a wonderful way to mitch from school with the approval of the authorities. It was at Yeats' Feis in Sligo that a softly spoken nun awarded prizes for the rendition of 'The Wild Swans at Coole' that brought the listener into the very feeling of being one of those swans. This poetry lark was turning into something that not even Batman or The Four Marys could boast of. A magical transmutation into any other being? It might be worth a try.

The same primary school encouraged all creative endeavour and love of the written word. Those were the days when *One Day in the Life of Ivan Denisovich* by Solzhenitsyn sat in rows of twelve on the shelf beside one rather battered copy of James Mitchell's *Jail Journal*. The days when the teacher encouraged you to try out for yourself what it was like to live on a crust of bread for a week. We were at the age when a fainting fit would afford you a rest from homework and the like. We were living the lives of the writers of whom we read. We visited Kilmainham Gaol, spelt with a 'G', and learned to venerate the poets who had died for their art. She may have said 'country', but I heard it as 'art'. It was time to enter the Allingham Poetry Competition, where I won second prize with my poem 'The Common Cold', the first verse of which runs as follows:

On opening a letter from the Medical Director
On the constitutional causes of the common communal cold,
A meeting was called of the surgical sector
On the constitutional causes of the common communal cold.

It didn't have the same effect as those early performances of 'An Old Woman of the Roads'.

And the medal was desperate, or perhaps I had outgrown the wearing of such gewgaws.

Secondary school focused on exams, and having not used the language that was true to me I gave up writing for a while, turning to it only now and then in times of teenage angst. But still it lured, leading me onward to read English Literature and Theatre Studies at Trinity. A new language enthralled me – that of prosody – and I was captured by the sublime paradoxes inherent in the using of forms that traditionally were utilised by men to speak to their beloved on lofty themes such as going to battle or not being able to live without the other. Thankfully, the adjudicator at Sligo was never forgotten, and I refused to internalise the lesson that there were only some things that you could be. After all, if you could transmute into a swan, you could be just about anything.

So I began again, tentatively at first, to write poems that assayed to be true to my voice and the voices of those I had chosen to use. The language I vowed to use would always be authentic, and would brook no use of it to make two girls kneeling on a linoleum floor feel in any way unimportant or disempowered. If there is a freedom to which one aspires now, it is of course that land where scapegoats are no longer thrown onto the refuse heap and discarded as being unworthy of poetic merit. For me, there is as much poetry in a prison queue, an acute ward or an outsider as there is in landscape, and the two can and do complement one another.

There were wonderful lecturers. Brendan Kennelly in particular championed my work, and got me a place in Annaghmakerrig, shortly after I graduated.

The theatre and its craft lured me for years, but during the time of the Celtic Tiger I reverted to my role as advocate and spent many years petitioning the courts for clemency on issues of eviction and reduction of sentences as a Community Worker. A new vision was gradually honed: one that had social justice at its core.

If that was the journey towards poetry on this side of the water, then it was a very different one on the other side. My ancestors here loved the written word, and many of them were poets in their own right or had devoted themselves to the word. My early childhood years are peppered with the memory of quotes I heard my mother say when the occasion merited it. It was all 'idea' over there. The idea of the land belonging to everyone, the right of common passage, the right to be equal, the right to go to Hyde Park and say whatever you wanted to say, and most importantly the idea that women were of course equal. No coyness here. The landscape took on different overtones. Fences and barriers were irrelevant. You could stroll over and through them, and that is a metaphor that I will carry with me for all my allotted time here on Earth. I had never before witnessed such joy at the production of a small handful of tomatoes. The passion for a pigeon, and the sense of ownership that the people I talked to felt. I carried this attitude with me over and back across the waters too, investing the bored ears of both sets of relatives with all my theories on land and language. How one said 'burd' here and said 'berd' there. The ballads I heard there, the folk songs and the lyrics here all transmuted into a burning flame that has never really expired.

As a result, I use sonnets, ballads, lyrics, prose poems and cinquains in my own work, borrowing from one tradition and bending it into the shape of the coats in which my own poetry is dressed. The themes are perhaps the themes that have attracted poets for millennia: those of love and loss, of pain and resistance, of hope and praise, of joy and ironic detachment, of death and illness. Sometimes the form I use is a direct commentary on that very theme.

I hope this collection of poems affords the reader the same pleasure I have had in crafting them, and if they fall short at times, in a slip of a word here and there, then so much the better. As the journey is a lifelong one, I would hope to improve. For those people who shared their lives and stories with me down through the years, who allowed me to walk with them in their struggle for equality and an equal place at whatever table they choose to sit, I thank them sincerely. I include among those the canon of both male and female poets who sit on my shelves like trusted friends.

In particular, I will always owe a great debt of gratitude to Nuala Ní Dhomhnaill for choosing my collection in last year's Listowel festival. She is a poet whose work I have always deeply admired. And I thank prosody, without whose language I would never have discovered a land where anyone can be anything, and where the best freedoms come from the shape, rhythm and metre of line length and sound. And I thank a poem called 'Bluebells' that I found in a drawer, written by my mother and secreted away, which led me to think that were other identities to which a woman could aspire.

Deirdre Hines, February 2012

The Listowel Collection

The Problem with Coats

lies in what cupboard you'll find yourself hanging
in whether you take them off
or keep them on.

They came from Persia's seamed fitters
along with the trouser
and settled as nouns –

I like to choose my coats
from the rails of second-hand shops.
Vincent de Paul is the best

for everything end of season.
I'd like to be my own designer,
but what of the other wearers?

the tailcoat met the lion-skin and called it savagery
the morning coat met the suffragette who called it inequality
the coatless met the landlords and called for democracy.

That's the problem with coats:
the way a simple naming can
switch them into scapegoats.

The only ones worth wearing
are the colour of two magpies clacking
from the top of rainbowed trees.

Black and Whites

If it has come to this, my love
that you and I are but the best
of friends, why then what was it all about?
What use is that to me in this lonely?
If we had known what it would do to us
the sneer and snide snickers would we have made
the leap into the void? We would –
I think like all the black and whites before
they took them all away run wild and free
Before one crow craawked danger, danger –
It matters and it matters not as now
is not the today of then; and cows
The chewing black and whites that can and do
what we had thought birthright not begged but due.

Demography

i am born my name is mary after the Blessed Mother
i have six sisters and the two brothers i am little i
have a horse i have five sisters and still the two
brothers i miss my sister may the saints and all the
blessed angels mind her up in the holy heaven i am
mary i am bigger now i live in Dublin that's the
capital sister of the country on a site like with no
toilets or electric or a Barbie shower or a binman I'm
going to the school and it's shite the school and the
teachers no I'm not going yes you are no I'm not me
mam won't let me layve I'm bigger now bigger than
youse lousers anyday me mam is crying over her
father that's my grandfather cos he's passed away
and he's only fifty lucky to reach fifty the others say
what's lucky about it there's a girl in my class and
she's a know-it-all pain in the arse Barbie bitch asked
me did i know that 5 in every 100 of our sort of
people pass 50 and a good job too says she and i
made a good job of her nose and I'm sispended and
that's a good job too best job ever the teecher said
I'm a creeminal elephant and what it has to do with
crayme and elephants i don't know and it just goes
to show the buffs the settled payple they're not near
wise i am mary i am bigger now i live in Dublin the
capital city of the country like i am blessed now i
made my communion the day there was a woman
came into our trailer the day me and me sisters we
say we we get a lot of visitors when i told me mam
that more payple visits us than visits the shrines and

the relics she told me for to shut my mouth we needs them payple i needs nothing from them and they aytes all the biscuits and they're nosier by far than the shades and that's the god's honest truth i am mary I'm ten years of age i have six sisters and one up in the holy heaven and two brothers and now the twins and they've just arrived the one a boy the one a girl so that's the seven sisters and the one that's up in the holy heaven and the three brothers and me mam's wore out and sos the rest of us and this woman came the day about the moving the moving into a house and she was saying that for every 102 of us who are boys there's only 100 who are girls me mam didn't know what she was on about and in her payple the settled payple there's 98.6 boys for every 100 girls and the next thing you know I says to me mam they'll be looking for our fellas and well i swear to the Blessed Mother and all the blessed angels they'll never get into my trailer to ayte all me biscuits and be nosing after me boys

Wishes
(for Dáirín)

Hoping
our teeth fell out
for fairy furniture
to swap for silver in eggcups
magic

in each
and every tree
moss mats and acorn hats
under every mushroom
gnome home.

Chasing
a cabbage white
who led us to a lane
between two high hawthorn hedges,
our camp

for those
two dearest dolls
Eileen and Annabelle
The carriage for contessas: that
red pram.

Snowdrops
in snow showers
the kitten born early
buried beside empty cottage
gardens

Searching
for mystery
under ivied headstones
found bone and plastic flowers to
treasure

against
Reason's growth –
before that time was spun
Sycamore keys were wings for flight
to lands

across
the sparkling seas
where children ruled
and adults were as extinct as
dodos.

Enchantment
(for Jimmy)

You were sitting on the shoreline
as I embraced white horses
jumping past the Nine Maidens;

The seven snails we stepped on
ghostwalk the sanded path
behind the Knavocks;

You strained to skyglide with hawks
hung in cloudless air
as I followed goldfinches

towards three stone stiles
that gifted early berries
and a while to pause

before five red ponies drummed
down empty fields
to chase us back

onto the spiral path
where webs caught drops
of dew in filaments

of light harvested like honey
against winter storms
in Fisherman's Cove;
in a dark and dripping cave

beams cannot reach
our treasured feathers;

pirate guardians light beacon fires
to spiritlure us back again
to Gwythian, oh Gwythian.

Boxrooms
(for Tishi)

In rooms like these begin the small revolts
Against the way it is, the way it was
Towards the way it could become only
If change can make inroads on all dead ends –
it's said to treat them mean to keep them keen,
it's said distance can make the heart so strong
the gap between what's said and is is wide
but just as hard to breach as breakers are:
Before she came in off the road to stay
against her will tethered to these white walls,
the sun and moon began and ended days
rhythms that held them close against the world –
the fault is when we try to be what we
are not and put others into a box.

Other Works

The Summering
(for Dad)

What words can paint the Summerings with her?
The scenes that form the lines of childhood run
amok among Slough markets, free to buy
white bags of pinky chew and sticks of rock.
All gone the dos and don'ts: I never could
In years to come, watch rose petals afloat
and not remember how we made perfume
a hoard against the winter snows and rains.
In my Nanny's garden flowers smell the
light air and planes flying overhead sound
the ear, all this before biscuits and juice
sparkly homemade elderpop that fizzed on
the tongue contrast to squash orange at home
that mocked my accent, my dress, my tone.

What is it that can draw me still to squirrels?
Squirrels in parks that run up trunks peeking
out at the two of us in matching
outfits with wicker trugs from which to feed
the reds and strays we met along the way.
The one we loved best selected Rich
Tea bits from your fingers so close and yet
So far like all the wild, living creatures.
"Hellos" and "How do you dos" replaced
Kalashnikovs and border checkpoints
Beside bordered beds of roses in the park,
One stray we met: his name was Dickens
He said he'd lost the path of life in war,
The one to save the star, the Number Two.

She knew the names of every herb, each tree
connected to the land, laneway and street:
a different way of mapping out terrain
not North and South but West and East as one-
The same with people too, who came and went
along the street, to peddle wares from door
to door, like leaves that leave their homes
for greener fields only to circle back
again always to her: the Summerings
undid corsets of belief, and we made
with rise and fall stitches outfits of pink
(not green or red and blue and white or black)
gingham to wear along high shoes from which
to dive and soar and view anew the land.

The game is photographic, trace the face
with fingers mouth to mouth and half-shut eyes
and memoriac: stories of trysts the best
the ones forbidden, in blitzed bunkers you
remaining to drive the milk in vans as trains
chu-chugged across the land into the West.
The well I threw pennies way down in Kernow
remembers as the stones remember us
petroglyphs the photos of old sacred altars:
Picasso said that pictures heal the sick
and you, and you also believed the two
of us in time and space had bent absence:
I heard the news by phone, pictured presence
In Summerlands ever and ever Summering.

Slawmeen Saturday

The bundle of twigs in the hearth
is a crow's nest that fell beneath
the broken grate –

Of the woman who at the window
used read the weather in the black clouds
above Nephin –

With the cattails of white smoke lit
from the yellow Argos, she used greet
another morning –

And from the old swing she watched
Daddy Joe seek lost "yirrols" hatched
on yellow hills –

The unpaid bills they used to put her away
so her meals could come on grey plastic trays
in the County Home –

Now the woman who at the window
used read the weather in the black clouds
above Nephin –

Hears strangers curse the blue mountain
for its interference with the televisions
in Castlebar –

Watches instead the Dublin road
where Mickey Joe sent a turf load
to help the war –

Hers was a visiting house, before
the phone lines came to shut the door
on dropping in –

And the cables broke the sound
of water lapping rock on strands
beside Lough Cullen –
As the poochers check their night-lines
a shooting star above blue Nephin
is the only sign –

But still there are those who swear blind
if you believe in places that bind
us to them –

The bundle of twigs in the hearth
is a soul's rest that fell beneath
the broken grate.

(A 'Slawmeen Saturday' is an untidy woman)

Valentine

a day like any other a day for lovers a day unlike any other and the sun is shining slanting and the church is packed rammed full of roses carried by the children a day like any other a day for lovers a day unlike any other and the sun is glinting glancing on the flowers and the wreaths on Best Mum, Best Daughter, Best Sister, Best Wife, and the roads that are closed and the screams they are bouncing back round the pillars and the pews and the crying childer and out the open doors up to the shining slanting glinting glancing sun, and she clayned the house and trailer and left no note before she took the tablets to take a trip to absence's shore and what they know for sure is the day she and the childer moved in off the road onto the road is there was terrible tauntings and the typical carry on from citizens and the like but what no one can know for sure is would they not have been better off away from there anyways and wasn't everyone depressed there and wasn't the worst of all loansharks with the hundred per cent interest there and didn't the drugs rule the roost there but wasn't there nowhere else to go but there, and now her ghost will haunt them all there so won't they have to go on from there and on the day they buried her in the graveyard on the hill above the town a day like any other a day for lovers a day unlike any other and the sun was glinting glancing on the guards in the blue trousers in and around the walls, in case of trouble there was double, on the hill

above the town with the mourners and the childer
and the guards in the blue trousers the shops and
bars were closed in case of trouble and everyone
had been warned on the day like any other a day for
lovers a day unlike any other on the hill above the
ghost town and what she knows for sure when she
rises from the grave is that she didn't know how to
read the labels and sure aren't all tablets the same
and sure the big talk of the doctors would put you
to the shame and sure isn't suicide a sin and sure
the town is even worse when you're on the other side
sure the doors are always closed even on a day like
any other a day for lovers a day unlike any other the
day they buried Bridie on the feast of Valentine.

Remember

Time has us in its grip
and we hold on until
the one or other of us
lets go, but echoes linger –

"that cat's a terror"
The morning the kitten
you were sitting for me
tumbled your garden –
the yoghurtpotporch.

"Time enough to grow up"
When it was time to gather hay
in the evening light all us children lay
across the towering stacks clinging
to yellow bits of stalks.

"Pink and green should never be seen, except in the
        washing machine"
You hovered like an exotic bird
gathering colours for your cupboard
blackberry, gooseberry, crabapple and damson
from John Callan's for your favourite jams.

"My mother, God rest her, loved that air"

Blown inland like the seagulls on the lawn
the squawk of waves brought you away from the
          farm
past the Five Crosses and Ballybay and Latton
to honeyed honeymoon Bundoran.

"Skinny Malinkey Long Legs, Big Banana Feet–"
Your breathless laugh shrugged names off
but you had the same grace as a newborn calf
a sense of wonder at it all,
a love of life.

"Well missus"
The treasure she hid for him was a letter
he found a year later in the drawer
on the landing beneath the Child of Prague
words from beyond to ease the loss.

"Well, mother, what's for tea?"
"Sure, you know what's for tea–"
Her words can move the curtains back
she's playing Hide and Seek: a trick
of the light is all her disappearance is
from this basket of eggs.

Hymn to a Goat
(For Rón)

Blessed be the day
the woman with dog-hairs on her coat
stood bargaining for a goat:
and you and I were flung
on the trip of a farmer's tongue
together again
at Foxford fair.

Blessed are you
the glee of the dance of you
the oh and the ah of the days with you
the three times three of the image of you:
In the mirrors of this room
in the barnhouse below Nephin
Pan multiplies.

Blessed is the goat
its worship of fire
its praise will not tire
Seen in eyes of gold
Heard in ears of hare:
but most of all, in all of us
It's mother to the unicorn.

Flight

Let's run through those three fields again
through the gaps in the bramble
across the stream and up the lane
into the wild, dark wood where bees bumble
wood voles mumble, pine needles tumble
onto the forest floor....
And sleep against the roots of an old oak tree
beside a hidden pool deep in the heart
of the green, wild and growing things and see
under a blanket of leaves, dappled darts
of light reflecting the sun as clouds part
in the waters of the pool....
And wake to starlight, rustlings in the ground
velvetwingflaps and two full moons
one above and one below and the mound
on the hill where the antlered deer soon
will gather to dance the ancient dance, boon
for the forest floor....
And run through those woods again
those wild, dark woods where bees bumble
wood voles mumble, pine needles tumble
onto the forest floor....
Down the lane and across the stream
and through the gaps in the bramble
and through those three fields
to dream of flight all over again.

Homo Sapiens

across the nightlawn
a hedgehog hunts slug slime trail
neighbours shoot the rat

Tiger

cerulean sky
fledglings fly wooden green gate
lighting my ghost cat

poverty

it's how much you own
how big your bank balance is
that tells your value.

wealth

donkeys rumpscratch bark
fields of yellow buttercups
in this junebloomroom.

Fragment 146

For me neither the sting
of the bee nor its honey
only the howl of the wolf
and the mewl of the cat
beneath a sickle moon.

For me neither the nectar
of honeysuckles nor the crackle
of popping hazelnuts
spelling out the sigils
of fortune's wheel.

For me neither the thorn
of the rose nor its sweet scent
only the wildflower meadow
and the roots of the dandelion
in the rocky crags.

For me neither the straight
road nor the winding path
only the labyrinthine labour
along the cliff edge
above star-speckled seas.

For me neither the tie
of threads tying and binding
me into a poppet doll
the oul' ones pull the strings of
around purple fires.

| Deirdre Hines |

For me only the call
of hidden hedges, lair of hare
where rutting stags bellow
and soaring eagles carry
me to freedom skies.

Bird's Eye View

Cast the gull's cold eye
On the image of him and you.
The report of wave and rock spells
A message on the strand.
If he is an island marooned in your well
And you are the sea banished from land:
You will not swallow his towered bell
He will not sink his root in your soft sand.
Cast the gull's cold eye
Cast the gull's cold eye...

Beneath the Holly Tree

I clear the earth beneath
the holly tree, shaking
slaters from rotted stumps.
I hear the cuckoo call
herald of bloom –
I plant the small, black seeds
Of blue forget-me-nots,
Your favourite flower.
In a Summer garden
beneath a holly tree
You taught me the secrets
of a woman's powering –
When he abandons me
as he abandoned you
I'll go and tend my young
green seedlings beneath
the holly tree.

My mind to me a kingdom is (Anonymous line from the English Renaissance)

His mind to him a warzone is
A metaphor of life
That cuts apart the lines and zones
To section out by strife.

The bombs he hears explode all day
Are real as real to him
The words he chants are age-old charms
To ward away the demons dim.

The prayer cards and candlelight
The meds he spits and hides
Weapons waged to fight
Against the March of rising ides.

But what is real and what is not
Isn't so plain or clear
The way we see the world is as
Habitual as fear.

But what if all we think we know
Is just the stuff of dreams?
Or worse, a sleight of hand, a trick
Nothing is what it seems.

Or does it all come down to webs?
An interconnect: worlds

Within and without; a game
Of catch and hold two birds.

Begun as quest across terrains
Where Magus Mesmer found
That trance could help to cure the sick
And light and even sound.

Charcot and Jung collected themes
In dreams and tales and art
Discerned mind patterns within
To integrate the heart.

The art of making things happen
To create worlds anew
Is now financial alchemy
And all is down to you.

Your mind to you your kingdom is
With all that it has been
But also all that it will be
A castle fit for queens.

Namings

what's your name again? clare, isn't it? – you don't have a cigarette spare do you clare somebody took mine thanks very much clare – it's what you'd call foundering out here isn't it?
do you know the village outside the town here, the protestant village with all the stone houses and the water well i live there and i'm sorry now i moved there clare aw for all sorts of reasons and it's got a bad name you know for not being friendly and the worst of it clare is that the top man here they call him the top man I'm sure you've heard of his name he got me moved down there so that he could stalk on me and look through my windahs whenever he felt like it you see they think they can do what they like just because of who they are, do you see like, and I was only making a cup of tea and some sandwiches when I sees him looking in at me and I had no choice then but to ask him in and ask him his name again, like I was only joking do you see what I mean like ,and he takes it all serious and says to me that there's a name for all this and i says to him so what i was only praying like and i was answering the priest like as if I was in my own church and so what if i wasn't they're watching me all the time like well we all genuflect... are you a catholic clare you are but your name's not clare don't worry about a name clare where was I? Oh yes i says to him no need to be going all high and mighty just because it's in his home place and he has his name to think of sure

don't we all have our names to think of and wouldn't i not be here with any name the day if my mother had listened to all the names they were putting on her in that other awful place that she escaped from many's a time God is God whatever your name is that's what I say don't you agree clare? He's the top man in here goes by the name of Doctor and he's very particular in that regard and he says i had to come down here to the town to this place and they haven't even put a name on the place yet but i'll be taking this up with the higher authorities because the way i see it he's the one with the delusions – the delusions of power – i only asked to go to the mass – sorry? you're only visiting the place and your name's not clare – never worry clare everyone in ireland has two names – the one they put on the people in here and the one God put on you when you were born – and the one they have on you in English and the one in Irish as well, like you know, belfast and béal féirste – are you from belfast clare? And you're not from Belfast and your name's not clare! don't worry about a name – they'll try to tell you names will never hurt you but never you believe them clare –

Tanka

Why a wounded wolf
is fighting phantasm foes
in an acute ward
is ancestral memory
howling for the wilderness.

| Deirdre Hines |

Lines Written At Pendennis Castle

When at Falmouth docks the line came to a halt
Like all those other endings; taste of salt
In the air, on my cheeks, in the seagull's cries
Up the steps, over the bridge, time flies
Around and in on itself; not straight as the arrow
In knight's tales of yore, but curved as the yarrow
Rooting between the ramparts of the castle keep
Threatening uproot of hurt stone deep.
How many times did I try to plaster over the walls
Of your scattered seed; only to crumble and fall
Away from fairystory into a wicker basket,
The willowed emblem of lies; flung in a casket.
The woman who makes a showcase of her heart
And head will live to see them break apart.

The Apple Man
(for Áilbhe)

There are many ways of saying it
but to cut to the chase
you'd like to upset his apple-cart,
knock him off his perch
and bring him down to size.

So you want to leave this world
and all its rotten apples
go somewhere where sunlight dapples
time, and everything is as it was
before your Eden fell –

But they'll say you have a screw loose
"What apples? What cart?"
No matter that the art
of apple-tempting is the centuries long cause
behind the conjugal excuse –

So this is what we'll do
us throwaways and discards
and no, it's not too hard –
We'll play a game of wait and see
We'll hire a lawyer who'll waive her fee,
We'll lobby for the rights of the wronged
We'll hire an assassin who's well armed,
We'll visit the local fortune teller
and buy a charm from her chrome trailer,
We'll kidnap him and sell him –

But what I hope for you is this
that you would take a knife
and in honour of your life
cut across the last apple
to find the five pips

shaped in a star –
and that you make a wish
upon it, that will banish
all fake apple-men from
your fair orchard –

and that you plant these five pips
in pots, beside your bedside
till you find that at your side
you have grown your own Green Man,
a real Apple-Man.

The Meeting Dance

On Mayday you had walked
the circle of me
a labyrinth of bloom:

In your eyes
the light fantastic gambols with
the wonders of Sun and Moon.

At Yule you had dissolved
the images of me
into beaks of prey:

In your heart
only the heron spearing to
the silence of the days.

At Bealtaine you had lost
the bearings of me
a fantasy blight:

In your hands
rot colours the tendrils of
the threads of night.

At witching hour I will gather
the traces of you
a heap for the cauldron:

In the waters of the well
two orangemarchmoons have spun
the story of you.

Mr Nothing

I thought

you were the bee's knees
and the cat's pyjamas –

You thought

you were the last word
and the one before that –

So you did.

You said

you were the cat's whiskers
the cream of the crop –

I said

You were the no one like you
the Something Special –

No one else did.

The oul' one says

The Mr Here I Ams
are always the Mr Has Beens –

When all is said and done,

That Mr Something is
Anything but

Nothing

would do you but
to have your Mr Nothing!

Wise Sayings

The throwaway line did it:
"She made her bed, so let her lie in it".

There's this thing about wise sayings
they're almost always wrong,

Not that we hunger for a bit of wise
grown like the river

Turning over pebbled beds
on her meander to the mouth.

But these hysterical times
favour unoriginal apophthegms

As honest as the cat when the meat is out of reach:
Sly rogues in good dress

That lie in wait in unexpected places
and spring their false and fickle faces

To trap us in deserted beds –
since when were words Truths?

The only beds of roses are the ones
bedded out with weeds

of the wild, less trodden paths
rooted in the river banks –

I plant bitter-sweet nightshade
that success may crown your wishes

And delicate blue harebells to
gift you courage –

And as I cast your lines
into the memorying waters

Remember this, oh wearied sister
You do not die of wisdom.

Future Perfect
(for JJ)

Outside
the churchyard wall
and tilting slightly now
a standing, solitary stone
so old.

Around
the russet hill
a grazing bullock saw
spray paint over the pictograms
young fools –

And yet
the lights that span
across early night skies
brought ancient artists to the stone
to dream

A child
of earth and stars
who speaks a future tongue
of breaking open sticks and stones
for peace.

Outside
the churchyard wall
and fallen over now
a standing, solitary stone
forgot.

Golden Calf

Thinking of you is to be warmed by Spring breezes
breathing awake the first bluebells on a March day
beside river-water, beneath the larch tree.

Dreaming of you is the feel of a panther's paws
the rise and fall of the velvet of you: black cat
starbathes on a sorrel bed behind iron gates.

Trying to land three white stones high above the sea
on Leac na Leannán, fulmars catch wishes in flight
thrown by a mooncalf on the cliffs above Tory.

Avalon
(pour le chevalier)

Full harvest moon rolls back jagragged clouds
Nightbreeze enchants with blackberried nutted air,
Digging the star map mirrored on the ground
In deep dripping lanes, badgers reveal lairs
Of beetles black and apples red and white.
Merlin's secret casts its spell; the springs are loud
One red, another white.

The Visit
(for Mum and Aunty Maura)

To spend a life and to have said you've spent it well
is not a question of bank accounts or lists you tick
off, of all done and yet to do-
when all is said and done there's much much more to us
than number...
                        but why then do we believe it all?
I knew a child who told me once in confidence
"only the God can count to fourever"

The physicists believe the past's a particle
and that what we've ahead of us is waves
perhaps that's true, perhaps it's not-
when all is said and done there's far far less to us
than placings...
                        so why then do we worship them?
I met a woman who told me once in confidence
"same plot but different characters"

The wars we wage are as varied as chalk and cheese
but much much more deadly, as power lures it bores
corrupts and turns against itself-
when all was said and done there's much much more to us
than hatred...
                        so why can't we crack the code?
My mother told me once in sympathy
"the   world's   more   full   of   weeping,   than   you   can
        understand"

Status is what we give the top dog lawyers, doctors
the   shrines   we   build   are   made   of   wordplay,   sticking
        plasters

that treat effects and ignore cause-
no matter how you dress it up or dress it down
the ladders
                    rule, circles were hit a sucker punch.
I loved a man who told me once in confidence
"Secrets are lies untold"

We close our ears but then visits that surprise catch
us unawares, reminds and jolts awake the soul
and what it takes to make it grow-
no matter where we run to or where we try to hide
it's there
                    valueless, weightless, waiting to go home.
I love the one who told me once in confidence
"You'll never be alone"